TAKE THE DYNAMIC WAY TO SUCCESS AND SPIRITUAL POWER

You have heard of—maybe even used—the technique called "positive thinking." That technique is based on creative visualization, which is an easy, effective method for tapping into the innate power of the mind. Some people apply visualization without actually knowing what they are doing, and achieve great success. However, many others prevent themselves from achieving their goals by wasting their time with wishful thinking and idle fantasizing—or worse, by envisioning failure. After you learn how to use the powers of creative visualization, there's absolutely no reason why you should be one of those unfulfilled people.

When you visualize for success, you first create an image in your conscious mind, then charge that image with the enormous psychic energy of your unconscious. It is possible to develop this completely natural power and apply it correctly—for your immediate and practical benefit. This book gives you the "big picture" on creative visualization, and illuminates the many ways this potent technique can improve your life.

The power of your mind is neither limited to nor limited by the material world ... in fact, *you* are the only thing keeping yourself from achieving whatever you're able to envision. *The Truth About Creative Visualization* is your key to your mind's amazing potential.

LLEWELLYN'S VANGUARD SERIES

The Truth About

Creative Visualization

by Keith Randolph

1995
Llewellyn Publications
St. Paul, MN 55164-0383, U.S.A.

For permissions, or for serialization, condensation,
or for adaptations, write the publisher.

FIRST EDITION
SECOND EDITION
First Printing, 1995

Cover illustration by Anne Marie Garrison

International Standard Book Number:
0-87542-353-1

LLEWELLYN PUBLICATIONS
A Division of Llewellyn Worldwide, Ltd.
P.O. Box 64383, St. Paul, MN 55164-0383

Llewellyn Publications is the oldest publisher of New Age Sciences in the Western Hemisphere. This book is one of a series of introductory explorations of each of the many fascinating dimensions of New Age Science—each important to a new understanding of Body and Soul, Mind and Spirit, of Nature and humanity's place in the world, and the vast unexplored regions of Microcosm and Macrocosm.

Please write for a full list of publications.

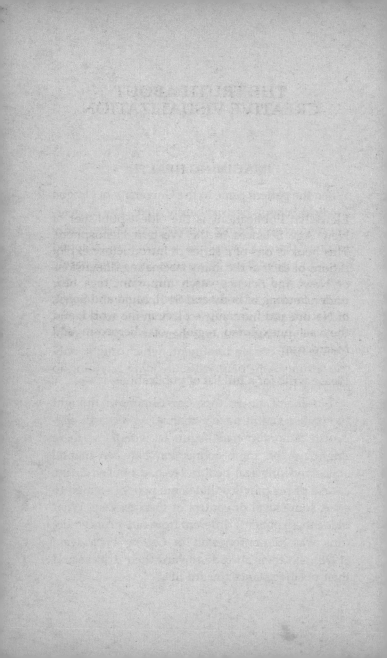

THE TRUTH ABOUT CREATIVE VISUALIZATION

IMAGINING HEALTH

When the patient came to the University of Oregon Medical School, he was barely alive. The 61-year-old man was suffering from a particularly deadly form of throat cancer. His weight had dropped from 130 pounds to 98 pounds. He could barely swallow, and could breathe only with great difficulty. Doctors who examined him gave him less than a five percent chance of living five more years. They even debated among themselves the ethics of giving him cancer treatment, which might only cause him more pain without doing anything to alleviate his illness.

But one of the doctors, Carl Simonton, thought the patient might have a chance. As a cancer specialist, Simonton had begun to wonder if there might not be some connection between mental states and physical health. He had noticed in the course of his practice that some people seemed to exert some level of control of their disease. What made these patients different from other cancer victims was, Simonton said in *Getting Well Again* (1978), "in their attitude toward their disease and their positive stance toward life."

Simonton had become sensitized to this curious phenomenon by his wife, Stephanie, a psychologist who had studied individuals who were unusually successful in life. Together the couple had studied various motivational techniques, and they learned that a principal component of them is the practice of visual imagery. In due course they started to wonder if such a practice could regenerate not only the spirit but the body as well.

The visual imagery process involves the individual's setting aside a period for relaxation, during which he or she conjures up a mental image depicting a desired result or goal. This exercise is done at least once a day, for anywhere from five minutes to half an hour. Whatever he or she wants to happen is envisioned as a consistent image (either literal or symbolic).

MILLIONS OF ENERGY BULLETS

Dr. Simonton took the patient aside and explained to him what he had in mind. He said he wanted the man to put aside three different periods a day lasting between five and fifteen minutes each. The first period started upon waking, the second at noon, and the third before bedtime. The patient spent each period sitting quietly and thinking of the muscles in his body. He would start at the head and go all the way to the soles of his feet, telling each set of muscles to relax. When this had been accomplished, he would be free of physical and emotional distractions.

Then he was to imagine himself in a pleasant place, perhaps under a tree by a quietly flowing creek. At that point he would think of his cancer, using whatever image he wished to symbolize it. Simonton then directed the man to think of his treatment, radiation therapy, as a million tiny bullets of energy piercing through every cell that came in their path. While the healthy cells would recover from this attack, the cancer cells would be too weak to repair themselves and would die.

The last image was to be of the patient's white blood cells swarming over the dead and dying cancer cells, carrying them off and flushing them out of his body through the liver and kidneys. At the conclusion of the vision, he would visualize his cancer as it continually decreased in size.

Simonton was astonished to witness what happened next.

The patient went through radiation therapy with practically no negative side effects. Soon he was eating again. His strength and weight returned. And the cancer disappeared.

He told Simonton that he had missed only one imagery session, and that had happened because a friend with whom he'd gone for a drive had gotten stuck in a traffic jam. This experience upset the patient because he feared losing control over his situation.

After two months of Simonton's mental-imagery program, plus conventional therapy, all signs of cancer were gone. Toward the end of the treatment, the patient told Simonton, "Doctor, in the beginning I needed you in order to get well. Now I think you could disappear and I would still make it on my own."

As if to prove it, he went on to treat other ailments from which he suffered. The first of these was arthritis, with which he had been afflicted for many years. In his mind he pictured his white blood cells smoothing over the joint surfaces of his arms and legs; as the cells passed over, they carried away debris, leaving the surfaces smooth and glistening. His arthritic symptoms declined. Although they still flared up from time to time, he was always able to diminish them so that they did not get in the way of anything he wanted to do, especially stream fishing—a rigorous sport even for those without arthritis.

Another problem he was able to overcome was impotence, which had effectively ended his sex life 20 years earlier. Using visualization exercises, he was able to resume full sexual activity within a few weeks.

Six years later, when Simonton described his patient's experiences in his book, he reported that the man's "condition in all of these areas has remained healthy for over six years."

VISUALIZATION WORKS!

Simonton emphasized that this story, while certainly dramatic, was hardly unique in his experience as a physician dealing with cancer patients. "Although it sometimes made no difference in the illness," he wrote, "in most cases it made significant changes in patients' responses to treatment."

Wanting to precisely and scientifically measure the effectiveness of visualization in cancer treatment, Simonton and his wife worked with a group of 159 patients, all diagnosed as suffering from medically incurable malignant cancer. All were expected to die within 12 months. Four years later, 63 patients were still alive; 14 of them exhibited no evidence of cancer; and 12 others were seeing their tumors shrinking. Even the patients who had died, however, had lived 112 times longer than patients in a control group not using visualization alongside medical treatment.

It should be emphasized here that the Simontons and their patients were not using visualization alone. It was being used in association with conventional medical treatment, whose effectiveness the Simonton's believed could be enhanced if combined with the kind of positive mental attitude visualization is intended to inspire.

In addition to relieving some of the physical distress of the cancer illness, Dr. Simonton found that visualization improved the general quality of the patients' lives. Many of the patients regained their energies so sufficiently that they resumed a level of personal activity comparable to what they had experienced before they got sick. As Simonton concluded his findings:

> An active and positive participation can influence the onset of the disease, the outcome of treatment, and the quality of life …. Expectancy, positive or negative, can play a significant role in determining an outcome. A negative expectation will prevent the possibility of disappointment, but it may also contribute to a negative outcome that was not inevitable.

SO WHAT'S NEW?

The Simontons had rediscovered one of the world's oldest systems of healing. It goes back at least as far as the ancient Egyptians. Hermes, the great Egyptian healer, believed physical diseases were caused by the mind along with the spirit and could be cured if the sufferer vividly visualized the operations of a healing god. Hermes believed that thoughts had vibrational and energy levels which could cause changes in the physical universe. First, however, one had to learn how to control and focus one's thoughts. Hermes' idea was so influential that it was later taken up by the Greeks, and still later by medieval physicians and healers.

The Greeks actually built healing temples which received pilgrims afflicted with all manner of illness. The priests who ran the temples would direct the guests to specially-designed sleeping rooms. There the guests would dream that the gods were instructing the patients to cure their diseases. Sometimes the dreams themselves were the cure. Apparently this technique worked; in the ruins of the ancient Temple of Epidaurus, archeologists have found records of "case histories" of patients who dreamed their way to health.

Paracelsus, the influential Renaissance physician who is considered one of the founders of modern medicine, was convinced that visualization was an effective way to treat an illness. He also thought that negative attitudes could cause diseases as surely as positive attitudes could cure them. "Man has a visible and an invisible workshop," he wrote.

> The visible one is his body, the invisible one is imagination (mind) ... The imagination is sun in the soul of man ... It calls the forms of the soul into existence ... Man's physical body is formed from his invisible soul.

Such ideas were revived in the late nineteenth century by Mary Baker Eddy, founder of Christian Science. Eddy wrote in her famous *Science and Health with Key to the Scriptures*:

> To prevent disease or to cure it, the power of Truth, of divine Spirit, must break the dream of the material senses. To heal by argument, find the type of the ailment, get its name, and array your mental plea against the physical. Argue at first mentally, not audibly, that the patient has no disease, and conform the argument so as to destroy the evidence of the disease. Mentally insist that harmony is the fact, and that sickness is a temporal dream. Realize the presence of health and the fact of harmonious being, until the body corresponds with the normal conditions of health and harmony.

SCIENCE AND THE MIND'S EYE

Until the 1920s, however, scientists considered such ideas no more than superstition or religious folly. The mind and body were believed wholly separate things, and it was considered absurd that mere thoughts might heal. Of course everyone knew thoughts could arouse the body sexually, excite fear or anger with a consequently faster pulse and heartbeat, and so on; but fight illness? Absolutely not!

But in the third decade of the twentieth century, J.H. Schultz, a German physician, created "Autogenic Training," in which patients sitting or lying in a relaxed state would imagine "mental contact" with the afflicted parts of their bodies. In effect, the patients were calling on their unconscious minds to aid them in the healing process. The technique, still in wide use throughout Europe as an adjunct to more conventional medical treatment, has been extensively studied and its effectiveness richly documented. Four separate studies, for example, showed that between 50 and 100 percent of asthma patients who practiced the exercises were able to alleviate all symptoms of the disease. Another study found that 70 percent of gastritis sufferers were significantly helped by autogenic exercises.

In the 1930s two medical researchers named Chappell and Stevenson worked with 52 peptic ulcer patients receiving identical treatment and dietary supervision. The researchers enlisted 32 members of the group in an experiment. Whenever they felt anxiety coming on, they were to visualize pleasant experiences.

Three weeks later the visualizing patients had no more ulcer symptoms. When dietary restrictions were lifted, all but one resumed normal eating habits with no further problems. The 20 patients in the control group, whose symptoms had been relieved only by conventional medical treatment, had their symptoms return as soon as they tried to eat normal food.

Although all 52 patients had suffered from ulcer problems for at least two years prior to the experiment, three years after the conclusion of the test only two members of the visualization group still had ulcer problems!

Another, rather more controversial, visualization-healing method was promoted by American opthamologist William Bates early in this century. Working from the principle that the act of seeing involves both a sense impression on the eye and the interpretation of that signal by the brain, Bates claimed, "When you can remember or imagine a thing as well with your eyes open as you can with your eyes closed, your vision will improve promptly." That's because, he said, a sharp mental image helps the eye to relax, assume its normal shape and send an impression the brain recognizes as sharper. "Perfect memory of any object increases mental relaxation, which results in a relaxation of the eyes, and both together result in better vision."

MIND OVER BODY

In recent years scientists have sought to document the idea inherent in all visualization-healing techniques that the mind can exercise control over the autonomic nervous system.

As early as the first decade of this century the noted British scholar and writer W. Y. Evans-Wentz visited Tibet and came back with incredible reports of what he had witnessed there. He said he had seen yogis sitting naked in the snow for hours at a stretch, and not only that, but the snow around them actually melted! The yogis told

Evans-Wentz that they were able to generate an enormous amount of body heat by visualizing a sun inside them.

Some years later, during the 1930s, a Soviet psychologist named A.R. Luria, along with associates at the All-Union Institute of Experimental Medicine, worked with a talented mentalist. The study involved a patient identified only as S. The study revealed S's abilities were greatly facilitated by his phenomenal ability to hold vivid mental images he had recorded years earlier.

But what really interested the scientists was his ability to increase his pulse rate from its normal 70 beats a minute to 100, and then to take it back to 70.

S said to the astonished investigators, "What do you find so strange about it? I simply sense myself running after a train that has just begun to pull out. I have to catch up with the last car if I'm to make it. Is it any wonder then that my heartbeat increases? After that, I saw myself lying in bed, perfectly still, trying to fall asleep ... I could see myself beginning to drop off ... breathing became regular and my heart started to beat more slowly and evenly."

The best scientific documentation of this ability was obtained in the 1960s by Elmer Green, head of the Menninger Foundation's Psychophysiology Laboratory in Topeka, Kansas. Green and his colleagues worked with Swami Rama, who demonstrated that through concentration he could change his body temperature, increase or decrease (and, in one instance, even stop) his heartbeat, and control his brain waves.

BACK TO LIFE

One of the more spectacular cases involving the use of visualization to change or repair the body is told by Evelyn M. Monahan, a writer and lecturer who in the early 1960s was involved in a serious accident. Her head was badly injured and as a result she went blind. Her doctors told her that nothing could be done. At 22, she faced the prospect of a life without sight.

But that was only part of it. Even worse was the fact that the same injury had turned her into an epileptic who experienced as many as a dozen seizures a day. Even with medicine, the attacks came 10 times daily. To further complicate things, four years later she suffered another accident. This one left her right arm paralyzed.

Perhaps understandably, Monahan felt pretty sorry for herself and became bitter and resentful. But finally, nine years after the initial accident, she decided to do something about her situation. She knew that conventional medical treatment had not worked, so she began reading about unconventional medical treatment. She learned about visualization techniques in which the afflicted person uses images designed to restore the body to health. Knowing she had nothing to lose, she vowed to try the techniques and asked two friends to try them as well, on the assumption that the psychic energies of three people were better than those of just one.

Ten days later Monahan's eyesight returned instantaneously. At the same time her epileptic seizures stopped. She went to her doctor, who ran several tests on her and found no further evidence of epilepsy. Soon afterward she stopped taking her medicine. "I have not experienced an epileptic seizure since that fateful day when my eyesight was returned to me," she wrote in her 1975 book *The Miracle of Metaphysical Healing*.

A week after the sudden curing of the blindness and epilepsy, she could move her right arm freely. The paralysis with its attendant pain had gone, never to return.

HEALING OTHERS THROUGH VISUALIZATION

A story like this verges on the miraculous, not only because of what it says about the mind's control over the physical body, but because of what it implies about the mind's ability to heal others. Monahan is convinced that her friends' visualizations were essential in her own healing.

After her own healing, Monahan vowed to teach others the techniques she had used. On a number of occasions she or her students even visualized healings for others. She describes the case of Mary C., whose 15-year-old son, Bobby, had been badly burned in an auto accident. In the first weeks of Bobby's hospitalization doctors had given him drugs to relieve his pain. The medication could have become addictive if continued, though, so it was stopped. His wounds were far from healed, however. When the pain returned, it came back with a vengeance. His parents listened heartbrokenly as he cried and screamed for someone to help him.

Mary C., who had heard of a healing course Monahan was teaching, called her. The two met soon afterward. Monahan outlined the visualization method that had helped her and the mother returned to her vigil at her son's bedside. She and her husband immediately began to imagine Bobby free of pain. Their son was well on the road to full recovery.

An hour later Bobby lapsed into peaceful slumber, the first real rest he had had in four days. In a few hours he awoke and spoke briefly with his parents before falling asleep again. "Mother, Dad, thanks for helping me," he said. "It doesn't hurt anymore. I'm just awful sleepy."

His parents continued to use visualization. In the weeks to come Bobby's recovery from his injuries proceeded with a rapidity that astonished his doctors. The physicians had concluded early on that several major skin-grafting operations would be necessary. As it turned out, it took only two minor operations to accomplish what had to be done.

PSYCHIC POWER OF IMAGES

Visualization, it appears, is a powerful psychic phenomenon. The energy it unleashes can work not only on the visualizer but on the outside material world. How can this be?

Parapsychologists have at least a partial explanation in the concept of psychokinesis (PK), popularly known as "mind over matter." Visualization exercises apparently help provide a focus whereby psychokinesis can be released from the unconscious mind to do its work. An instance was demonstrated in July of 1977 at the Science Unlimited Research Foundation, a parapsychological laboratory in San Antonio, Texas.

Dean Kraft, one of America's leading psychic healers, was the subject of the experiment. The scientist who had devised the test, Dr. John Kmetz, wanted Kraft to kill cancer cells grown in specially designed culture flasks.

Parapsychologist D. Scott Rogo writes in *Exploring the Healing Miracle*.

> Kmetz chose an exceptionally virulent cancer cell, the HeLa, for the experiments. These cells are grown in flasks and stubbornly cling to the bottom. Not even vigorous shaking will dislodge them. The cells detach only when they die, whereupon they float freely in the solution.

Kmetz wanted to see if Kraft could increase the number of dead cells in the solution by merely focusing his healing powers on the culture. The dead cells can be counted by a hemacytometer, so an objective determination could be made by running counts before and after Kraft focused on the culture. A total of six identical experiments with the HeLa cultures were undertaken over a three day period.

In his autobiography, *Portrait of a Healer*, Kraft describes what happened next:

Concentrating on the picture I'd formed in my mind of the cells, I directed my thoughts to the flask and visualized a disturbance in the cell fields and the cells blowing up ... After about 20 minutes, I knew that I'd affected the cells. I sensed a definite interaction, almost a magnetic pull, between my hands and the flask.

After the test, researchers counted a 200-percent increase in the number of dead cells. When Kmetz studied the dead cells under a microscope, he was struck by their appearance. It looked as if they had exploded internally.

Psychic healers employ visualization not only to treat illnesses but also to diagnose them. Among the Navahos, for example, clairvoyant visualization is central to traditional healing techniques. However, the healer and the diagnostician are two separate persons. The "hand trembler," as the latter is called, is brought in to find out what the patient's medical problem is. He goes into a trance and during a ritual ceremony visualizes the affliction. The "singer," or shaman, then comes in and visualizes the treatment (frequently the proper mixture of herbs).

CAYCE'S CLAIRVOYANT VISUALIZATIONS

The most famous clairvoyant visualizer of all time is probably Edgar Cayce (1877-1945). Cayce would go into a light trance and clairvoyantly diagnose illnesses of people he did not know or had not even met. Thousands of people were helped by the man who became known as the "Sleeping Prophet."

One of them was a man we'll call Jack Bedford. Bedford, a resident of New York City, was a post-office foreman who, with no history of mental illness, suddenly began to develop severe pains in his head. His behavior became erratic, and he had periods of amnesia or irrationality. He grew ever more depressed and irritable and finally his emotional condition cost him his job.

At last Bedford was declared incurably insane, and he was committed to Rockland State Hospital in Orangeburg, New York.

His family and relatives were devastated by this turn of events. To them the whole affair was a dark and terrible mystery. How could this decent, hard-working man have inexplicably fallen victim to overpowering mental illness? But the doctors just shrugged their questions off. They said there was nothing that could be done, and that Bedford's family should just get on with their lives.

Then Bedford's sister remembered something a former employer had told her about a man named Cayce. In some miraculous way, Cayce had helped a young Southern woman recover from mental illness. So Bedford's sister called her former employer, a businessman named David Kahn, who happened to be a friend of Cayce's. That night Kahn wrote the psychic, saying only that the man "had a nervous breakdown ... He is in Rockville State Hospital ..."

A few days later the sister received a typewritten note, dated January 7, 1938. It was from Cayce, who offered this diagnosis:

> Through pressures upon nerve energies in the coccyx and the ileum plexus, as well as pressure on the lumbar axis, there has been a deflection of the coordination between the sympathetic and the cerebrospinal nervous system.

The note said that the problem was caused by a fall on the ice Bedford had suffered as he was leaving work one day three years earlier. Cayce accurately described the treatment Bedford was getting at the hospital and went on to say which parts of it were worthwhile for the problem and which were not. Bedford "is not insane," Cayce said. "He does not belong in an institution." He concluded by prescribing certain osteopathic methods of healing Bedford's affliction.

"WE HAVE THE BODY ..."

Cayce arrived at this diagnosis as he arrived at all his diagnoses: "by seeing it psychically."

After he got Kahn's letter describing Bedford's plight, Cayce retired to his study and lay down on a leather-covered couch. As his wife, secretary and two visitors sat nearby, he closed his eyes and went into a trance. Soon he started to speak, saying, "Yes, we have the body ..." Next he related what he visualized—all of it, including the diagnosis, which was startlingly accurate. The letter Bedford's sister later received was a transcript of his trance remarks.

Kahn secured the services of a sympathetic physician who was willing to employ the unconventional treatment Cayce had proposed. Six months later Jack Bedford was a well man, out of the mental hospital and back to work at the post office. Cayce biographer, Vaughn Shelton, wrote:

> The list of Edgar Cayce's miracles is breath-taking. His own wife was cured of advanced tuberculosis; a Catholic priest in Canada was cured of epilepsy; a young woman was cured of scleroderma, which turns its victims to stone; a man in New England was cured of arthritis; a woman was cured of intestinal fever. The thousands of cures cannot be listed. But each case is documented with the origi-

nal, witnessed reading and the written statements of the attending physician, the patient, his family and other interested parties.

IMAGES OF ESP

In recent years parapsychologists have conducted extensive research into what Charles Honorton, a pioneering investigator in this area, calls "internal attention states." Honorton and others have shown that ESP can be significantly enhanced if the subject's mind is free of all distractions and solely focuses on mental images that arise spontaneously from his unconscious.

Their research is being done with "ganzfeld" stimulation (Ganzfeld is a German word meaning "homogenous field.") In a typical experiment, the subject lies down, and the experimenter covers his eyes with halved ping-pong balls. Next the experimenter places earphones over the subject's head and, the sound of undifferentiated static ("white noise") comes through. The experimenter leaves the room.

Elsewhere another person, called an "agent," directs telepathic signals to the subject, who is describing the mental images he is "seeing." Later those mental images are compared to the ones the agent sent. Parapsychologists have found that the two sets of images are often strikingly similar, suggesting that telepathy has been at work. They also learned that even people who had never had psychic experiences before had no trouble receiving the telepathic signals sent to them.

But scientists doing ganzfeld experiments discovered a strange psychic effect for which they were totally unprepared. It turned out that some subjects were picking up the images BEFORE the agent sent them. In other words, they were not reading somebody else's mind—they were looking into the future!

As the ganzfeld work has continued, another surprising fact has come to light. People who have participated in repeated experiments get better and better at it—in other words, become more psychic—and their new talents also manifest OUTSIDE the laboratory, in their daily lives.

VISUALIZATION BEYOND THE BODY

In traditional cultures the shaman functions as healer and seer. His role is to mediate between the material world and the spiritual world. When someone requests a healing, the shaman visualizes his soul traveling through other realms of existence seeking the patient's soul. When found he returns it to the sufferer and a healing is accomplished.

Visualization has long been seen as a key to the out-of-body experience (OBE), also known as "astral projection." Occultists teach ways to induce the sensation of separation of consciousness from the body, and many involve intense visualization exercises. For example, before a student is given instructions in the specific techniques of astral projection, the student may be directed to visualize a room or a picture repeatedly, until every single detail of it stands clearly and vividly in the mind. Once the student has brought his or her visualization skills to a peak through this sort of exercise, the student proceeds to OBE visualization.

A common OBE technique has a student sit in a half-darkened room, close his or her eyes and imagine himself or herself sitting in a distant corner. Or the student may imagine a duplicate self standing nearby. Another method teaches a student to lie down and "see" himself or herself rise into the air until all awareness of the bed passes; then the student visualizes himself or herself standing at the foot of the bed gazing down on his or her physical body. The object is for the student to eventually really leave his or her body, not just imagine doing so. The goal is for imagination to become reality through constant practice—which, incidentally, is the principle underlying ALL visualization techniques.

THE MAN WHO BECAME A LIGHT BULB

In his *Handbook of Astral Projection*, Richard A. Greene discusses an OBE-producing visualization exercise calling for the practitioner to "transfer ...

consciousness into any object and try to see from the object's point of view."

One person who tried this technique successfully describes how he attempted to transport his consciousness into a light bulb hanging from the ceiling on the opposite side of the room. Initially he had the sensation of "bouncing back and forth between my body and the light bulb." Just as he would feel himself centered in the bulb, he would start to reconstruct the structure and appearance of the room. This "intellectual" effort, which drew on memory rather than direct perception, inevitably put him right back into his body. He assumed all the while, however, that these "events" were occurring solely in his imagination.

Then one day he realized that imagination had fused into reality. As he visualized himself inside the light bulb, he looked down from his vantage point into two boxes. He had known all along that they were there, but he had never bothered to examine their contents. But now he "saw" that one box contained wire and the other scraps of paper. ("The word 'seeing' to describe the way I saw these things is not the right word," he says. "They were images which penetrated into my consciousness. Along with the perceptions came a solid feeling of their being totally and completely right.")

He immediately willed his consciousness back into his physical body and went to view what was inside the boxes—to discover what his "imaginary" visualized perception had already told him. More-over, when he physically positioned himself close to the light bulb, he found that the perspective was exactly correct, down to his being able to detect cracks and scratches in the wall not visible to one standing on the floor looking up. In short, he real-ized that now he was no longer just pretending to leave his body; he WAS leaving his body.

A psychologist experimenting with visualization had no idea that he would generate real OBEs when, as part of an effort to help his students exercise con-trol over their mental experiences, he di-rected them to imagine they were traveling into outer space. Sev-eral of his students told him that while they were visualizing such a trip, they suddenly left their bod-ies and underwent classic OBEs. The psychologist, Sandor Brent of Wayne State University, was so impressed that he overhauled his program and made it a formal exercise for inducing group OBEs!

FROM INNER SPACE TO OUTER SPACE

In Brent's program, students gather in a relaxing at-mosphere, either sitting in comfortable chairs or lying on the floor, while the lights are dimmed to ensure a minimum of distractions.

Members of the group are encouraged to talk with one another so that they can develop a sense of trust and comradery. Then the group leader (sometimes known as the "tour guide") takes over.

He explains that the participants are about to experience a "mental world" that exists outside them and is as real as the physical world. He points out that purely physical perception is extremely limiting, and affords human beings only a tiny view of a larger cosmic reality. We demand that all reality conform to our expectations of what it is and of what it consists. But participants in the experiment are able to break out of that tiny perceptual corner and explore other ways of seeing.

The first exercise involves the transference of consciousness to different parts of the body. Participants visualize their conscious selves in their feet, abdomen, hands, shoulders or elsewhere in their anatomy and for a time "see" everything from those vantage points. In due course, consciousness moves upward to the head. Next, participants scan their bodies seeking tense areas. When they find them, they "release" the tension until at last their bodies are totally relaxed.

At this point the guide directs the subjects to release their consciousness by projecting it through the tops of their heads. Participants stand outside their bodies and observe them carefully; then they move on to leave the room and the building. The leader instructs them to rise into the air and to examine the landscape beneath them, and will eventually direct them into outer space. The "trip" ends when the guide tells participants to visualize themselves entering a great void or white light.

In his early experiments Brent was disconcerted to learn that some of his students weren't "coming back." They were either intensely absorbed in the experience or literally could not find their bodies. Some reported classic near-death experiences (in which, typically, the participant found himself entering a realm of beautiful, overpowering white light and encountering discarnate or angelic beings). Brent had to devise additional steps to help his participants retrace their psychic footprints until they located their physical selves and merged with them.

VISUALIZATION POWER

The point we are making here is that visualization is an extraordinarily powerful instrument. In focusing our psychological and psychic powers and drawing on the untapped potential of the unconscious, we are dealing with forces that in some ways seem almost magical. One writer on visualization, Robert Hezzelwood, speaks of the "wizard within":

> Distracting the attention of the conscious mind, or focusing it on the desired result, combined with some form of inductive relaxation, opens the doors to the transmitting capabilities of the psyche. When the transmitter has been 'warmed up,' one can then implant the suggestion or image on the transmitted waves; if the transmitter is strong enough it will affect what we normally consider objective reality.

Paul Ellsworth learned visualization techniques early in life and continued to practice them over the years until he became quite proficient. The more skilled he became, the more spectacular were his successes with visualization. One such success came about during a crisis in Ellsworth's professional life.

Ellsworth worked as a writer for a trade journal, and liked his job. A managing editor unjustly suspected that Ellsworth was after his job. The manager made things as difficult as possible for him. Finally he had Ellsworth fired.

Ellsworth went home and devoted all his energies to a visualization exercise he hoped would help him out of his problems. First, he read metaphysical books and devoted much conscious thought to his professional, personal and psychic potential. When he felt ready, he relaxed for the next 10 to 15 minutes and focused on a mental image of himself as prosperous and successful.

BLAST OF PSYCHIC ENERGY

Two minutes later Ellsworth's phone rang. When he answered, he was surprised to hear his former superior's voice.

The voice was shaking. He asked Ellsworth if he would take a train, at company expense, to the home office 200 miles away and join him the next morning. He wouldn't say what had happened, but alluded that it was very important.

When Ellsworth walked into the office, his ex-superior told him that the previous afternoon (just at the time, Ellsworth realized, he had been lying on his bed doing visualization) the owner of the company, a man of vast money, power and influence, had abruptly entered the office. The editor was astounded; he had not even known the owner was in town. Besides, the man owned so many companies and investments that the trade magazines were of relatively little concern to him. Many employees who had worked on the magazines for years had never actually seen the man.

The first words the tycoon uttered were, "What are you doing about Ellsworth?"

Thoroughly shaken, the editor mumbled something, to which the owner responded by directing him to make an immediate phone call to Ellsworth and get him to the office the following morning. No one ever knew how it had 'happened,' Ellsworth related in an article in FATE.

> I would have liked to know the sequence of events. But I never did. All I knew was that this multi-millionaire took over my affairs for several years, pushed me ahead in one or another of his organizations, told me through his confidential man that he meant to make my fortune. He failed only because a time came when I got the old gypsy feeling and moved on.
>
> But the blast of psychic energy turned into my life that afternoon continued to dominate

my life for 10 years. Whatever I did I prospered, people who could do things for me hunted me up—sometimes they were persons I had never heard of.

PRECOGNITIVE VISUALIZING

Sometimes there is an element of precognition (the ability to foresee the future) in visualization. The image the visualizer conjures up may not be from his imagination, as he thinks; it may be a glimpse of an actual physical environment or situation he will experience at some point in the future.

Harold Sherman, who frequently writes on the psychic power of visualization, recounts the experience of a Pennsylvania couple of his acquaintance. Mr. and Mrs. B. had lived in a large city for many years but had always wanted to move to the country. After reading one of Sherman's books on imaging, Mrs. B. decided to apply the technique in a very specific way.

She would look out her kitchen window onto the city scene outside and declare, "The apartment houses over there are really the Blue Mountains. I will look out over the Blue Mountains while I'm doing my dishes."

She went on to describe more of the environment in which they would be living once they moved to the country.

> Our house will sit back off the road ... It will be on a small hill or mound ... and the street down there will be an old dirt road," she told

her husband. She pointed to the spot where a brook would be and she went on to tell what the other buildings on the property would look like.

Every day I visualized, every day I looked at the 'mountains' as I did my dishes," she wrote to Sherman. "Every day I passed my 'brook'; every day, coming home from work on the busy street, I was really walking up my 'road' ...

My husband and I pictured our home so vividly that it is EXACTLY what we got!

They ended up living in the Pennsylvania Dutch country. From her kitchen Mrs. B. saw in reality the Blue Mountains just as she had "seen" them in her imagination. The brook, the house on the hill, the other buildings were all as she had "imagined."

Every evening I take my stroll around the beautiful valley; down the old dirt road. In the city I had visualized the trip to the store in the evenings as I am doing now.

Parapsychologists know that precognitive visions typically appear spontaneously from the unconscious or manifest in dreams. The kind of experience Mrs. B. recounts is unusual, although certainly not unheard of. The psychic forces that can be unleashed in visualization often work in a surprising and astonishing fashion.

A SENSE OF DIRECTION

Visualization doesn't always manifest that dramatically, of course, and it is not solely a psychic phenomenon whose effects are accomplished through telepathy, clairvoyance, astral projection, precognition or psychokinesis. It is much more than that.

Visualization forces us to communicate with our own deepest selves. It enables us to know who we are, not who the world says we are. By relaxing, shutting out all distractions and concentrating our attention solely on ourselves, we leave nothing between us and our psyches. Whatever we draw out of our unconscious, and whatever we put back into it, is indisputably ours. The images involved in this dialogue between the conscious and unconscious minds are powerful and true; they are pure and undiluted. They are us in our most profound sense.

Moreover, the images we conjure up or experience during visualization are not forgotten or discarded as we return to normal consciousness and go about the mundane business of our lives. The images are stored in the unconscious, where they remain powerful forces. The images act on our conscious minds even when we are unaware they are doing so. This is especially true if in visualization exercises, we continue to return to them and thereby "recharge" them. As Paul Ellsworth puts it:

Some novices have tenderfoot luck and pro-
duce genuinely miraculous results very early.
Others have to work longer. But there is a
cumulative effect in this kind of work. The
energy builds up, as if you were charging a
Leyden jar. 'Drop by drop the pitcher fills.'
When it is full, it brims over into your miracle.

The "miracle" is accomplished because visualization causes you to focus your scattered emotional energies. It gives you a vivid image of what
you want, and this image becomes a symbol of
what your life is about. To bring that image into
the reality of the material world, your unconscious mind uses every power at its disposal.
Sometimes this power manifests as psi. More
often it works by directing your daily attitudes
and activities toward the achievement of the goal
you envision. Everything you are doing, whether
you realize it or not, is pushing you in the direc-
tion you want to go.

Not only are you working harder and more con-
fidently, but you are more keenly sensitive to the
most subtle events in your environment. You are
tuned into coincidence, into opportunity in unlikely
places, and any other circumstance that will bring
your mental image into flesh-and-blood, nuts-and-
bolts reality.

SEEING AND BELIEVING

As Claude M. Bristol puts it in his famous book *The Magic of Believing*, "The person with a clear goal, a clear picture of his desire, or an ideal always before him, causes it, through repetition, to be buried deeply in his subconscious mind and is thus enabled, thanks to its generative and sustaining power, to realize his goal in a minimum of time and with a minimum of physical effort."

Norman Vincent Peale, well known as a clergyman, writer and advocate of "positive thinking," has told of how he discovered the power of "positive imaging." Some years ago he and his wife Ruth started an inspirational magazine called *Guideposts*. They had started it on a financial shoestring but had some early success, attracting about 40,000 subscribers before money ran out. The magazine's demise looked all but inevitable.

The Peales called a meeting of the board of directors. It was a gloomy gathering. Debts were high and spirits low—until a woman named Tessie Durlack spoke up.

"The situation," she said, "is that you lack everything—subscribers, equipment, capital. And why do you lack? Simply because you have been thinking in terms of lack. You have been imaging lack so, therefore, you have accordingly created a condition of lack. What you must do now, at once, is to firmly tell these lack thoughts or images to get out of your minds. You must start imaging prosperity instead."

The directors objected that this sounded like an invitation to lose themselves in unreality, but the woman, clearly impatient with their lack of faith, quoted Plato's admonition to "take charge of your thoughts. You can do what you will with them." She ordered every one to "flush out these lack thoughts, and do it now."

So as the directors sat there, they imagined that they were flushing the thoughts out and "seeing" them march out the door.

THINKING PROSPERITY

Then Durlack, obviously a woman of firm and commanding presence, directed the group to start thinking of images of prosperity to replace the old ones of debt and failure. She stressed that if these positive images were let out of mind, they would quickly be replaced by the old negative images.

She asked how many subscribers *Guideposts* needed to have in order to continue publishing. The directors estimated that it would take 100,000.

"All right," she declared, "I want you to look out there mentally and see or visualize 100,000 persons as subscribers to *Guideposts*, people who have paid for their subscriptions."

So the group sat, concentrated and soon "saw" the subscribers. "Now that we see them," Durlack went on, "we have them." Then she had them pray to thank God for the 100,000 subscribers he gave them!

The Peales were so struck by the power of this introduction to visualization that they half-expected to look over at the table of unpaid bills and find that they had disappeared. Of course that didn't happen. What did happen, though, is that the board of directors came to life, enthusiasm returned, and this brought renewed confidence and creativity. Soon they were batting new ideas back and forth.

In the months that followed, all those connected with the magazine kept the positive images uppermost in their minds and did not let themselves consider the possibility that their confidence in a happy future was misplaced. In a short time, the bills began to dwindle. The subscription rate rapidly rose. With amazing swiftness the goal of 100,000 subscribers was reached—and surpassed. Today *Guideposts*, with over 3½ million subscribers, is one of the largest magazines published in the United States.

There is nothing necessarily "supernatural" about this little incident. The visualization exercise helped free the creative potential needed to keep the magazine alive. It also unleashed basic emotional and physical energies that had been paralyzed by the sense of hopelessness associated with what looked like imminent failure. Yet the effect of this psychological liberation was so overwhelming that, in a way almost "magical," it affected the material world.

SPORTS VISIONS

Although the fact is not well known, visualization plays a key role in the successes of many great athletes. Most obviously, of course, visualization increases confidence and motivation. Less obviously, it affects and sharpens players' muscles.

This was discovered by physiologist Edmund Jacobson when he had subjects visualize certain athletic activities. Through the use of sensitive detection instruments, he discovered subtle but very real movements in the muscles that corresponded to the movement the muscles would make if they were really performing the imagined activity.

Further research revealed that a person who consistently visualizes a certain physical skill develops "muscle memory" which helps him when he physically engages in the activity. A related study by Australian psychologist Alan Richardson confirmed the reality of the phenomenon.

Richardson chose three groups of students at random. None had ever practiced visualization. The first group practiced free throws every day for twentieth days. The second made free throws on the first day and the twentieth day, as did the third group. But members of the third group spent 20 minutes every day visualizing free throws. If they "missed," they "practiced" getting the next shot right.

On the twentieth day Richardson measured the percentage of improvement in each group. The group that practiced daily improved 24 percent. The second group, unsurprisingly, im-proved not at all. The third group, which had physically prac-ticed no more than the second, did twenty-three percent better—almost as well as the first group!

In his paper on the experiment, published in *Research Quarterly*, Richardson wrote that the most effective visualization occurs when the visualizer feels and sees what he is doing. In other words, the visualizers in the basketball experiment "felt" the ball in their hands and "heard" it bounce, in addi-tion to "seeing" it go through the hoop.

A PSYCHIC EDGE?

As in other activities drawing on the power of visual-ization, sports feats are sometimes assisted by para-normal aspects of the mind. Parapsychologist Rhea A. White, for example, is convinced that the best athletes have what she calls a "psychic edge." Their intense concentration/visualization of what they seek to do brings psychokinesis into the equation.

Jack Nicklaus, the great golfer, says that "will power is what separates the great athlete from the average to mediocre athlete." He points to his cele-brated colleague Arnold Palmer who, when putting, would "see" the ball go into the hole and "will" it there. Ben Hogan, another major figure in golf his-tory, said once that if he concentrated hard enough on where he wanted the ball to go he could put it there.

The controversial Israeli psychic Uri Geller claims that as a teenager he spent hours shooting baskets and he writes in his autobiography, "It intrigued me that, when the ball rolled anywhere on the rim, it would inevitably drop in if I concentrated on it; it would also seem to vary slightly in its course if I concentrated … "

In football, New York Giants tight end Gary Ballman tells how he came to make an impossible catch. Another player had thrown the ball to him but had overthrown it badly; there was no way he could possibly retrieve it. But Ballman wanted the football so much that he imagined it slowing in its flight and dropping into his hands. To his utter astonishment, that is precisely what happened. "It was a strange feeling, I'll tell you," he said.

These kinds of odd events are hardly uncommon. White, a sports fan who has conducted an extensive investigation of the phenomenon of PK in athletic contests, says:

> Competitive sports demand a great deal of the participating athletes. They must be strongly motivated, employ intense concentration yet remain relaxed, visualize their targets and drive themselves beyond the normal limitations of their muscles. It shouldn't seem strange, then, that some of these athletes, as they psyche themselves up to this extra mental and physical output, are using PK.

THE POWER OF NEGATIVE THINKING

So far we have been considering visualization as a technique that works because it forces us to concentrate all our energies, psychological and psychic, on positive images. We have seen visualization as a method of transcending the many negative forces that distract and bedevil us. But what about NEGATIVE imaging? Does that work too? The answer is yes and no.

Yes, it is possible to focus on a harmful or unethical goal and to bring that goal into material reality. But it is a dangerous business, because negative imaging unleashes the destructive elements of the unconscious. On the other hand, positive imaging draws forth the constructive elements. As we have noted repeatedly, once tapped, the powers of the unconscious can be overwhelming. Negative imaging can destroy you.

Some years ago a famous Hollywood producer made an appointment with a psychiatrist. He told the doctor that his life was in ruins, his career was going badly, he couldn't sleep, he couldn't think straight, and so on. Eventually the whole story came to light.

The producer had met an attractive young actress who was struggling to get started in the movie business. Although married, the producer set about trying to seduce the woman, who had resisted his advances. The man, who knew about visualization, began practicing imaging exercises in which he imagined the entire process leading up to his goal of bedding down the actress. Things turned out just as he had imagined them—up to a point.

The woman got pregnant. She thought that the producer loved her and that he would divorce his wife and marry her. When she came to him with the news of her condition, he was appalled. He ordered her to get an abortion. Instead she went back to her apartment, swallowed a large number of sleeping pills and died, leaving a note revealing just what had happened. The resulting scandal destroyed the producer's career.

Positive visualization works because positive images seek out positive forces in the outside world. When the mental and physical worlds are in harmony, the results can be explosive. Negative visualization draws on negative forces, with predictably catastrophic consequences.

POSITIVE NEGATIVE IMAGING

Of course, it is possible to draw on negative imaging in pursuit of a positive goal.

One morning an alcoholic, unable to cure the disease that had broken up his family, caused him to lose his job and devastated his life in every way, awoke in Bellevue Hospital in New York City. He was very sick and miserable. All around him were people whose lives alcohol had destroyed. The scenes of human wreckage all around him were horrifying.

"I'm in hell," the man thought. "If I could just remember exactly how I'm feeling now, how ashamed I am, how utterly horrible all this is, I would never take another drink."

Upon his release he kept thinking of the phrase "If I could just remember ... " And so he decided to remember—every day. Every day he vividly visualized the scenes he had witnessed in the alcoholic ward and relived every terrifying, sordid detail. He was convinced that in so doing, he could get through the day without taking a drink. He was right and was permanently cured.

This story demonstrates the power of imaging in overcoming our destructive impulses. Happily, most of us are not in the grips of acute alcoholism, but we all have bad habits. We all do things that serve no constructive purpose, that at the least waste our time and at the worst keep us from doing what we need or want to do.

A writer who found the business of composing words and sentences a tedious, wearying process had an enormously difficult time disciplining himself to sit down in front of the typewriter and attend to his work. He was continually finding excuses not to work, and was always distracted by personal problems or by other, more pleasant pursuits. In due course, he became almost totally unproductive, and his professional life suffered accordingly.

Finally a friend suggested he try visualization exercises. The writer did some reading on the subject and, although somewhat skeptical, decided to give it a try. Several times a day he imagined a photograph of himself. In the photograph he was smiling, a man clearly at ease with himself and happy in his life. The writer mentally described the man in the picture (himself) as a fellow who worked hard as a writer and, what's more, enjoyed working hard. The man in the picture was prosperous, successful and had reaped all due reward for his hard work.

Within a matter of days the writer was back at the typewriter. He found he wanted to work and only became impatient or distracted when he wasn't working. His output soared. His writing improved and he was startled to find that he actually began to like to write. His career, which had been moribund during his long period of paralysis and inactivity, suddenly became very successful, with new opportunities presenting themselves at an almost dizzying rate.

VISUALIZING FEAR AWAY

Psychologists and psychiatrists increasingly make use of visualization techniques to deal with patients' fears and anxieties. Two psychiatrists independently devised methods of using negative imaging for positive purposes.

One of them, A. Beck of the University of Pennsylvania, has described his work with a man who was troubled by uncontrollable fantasies about being in a car as it crashed into a wall. Whenever the image appeared in his imagination, the patient would be overwhelmed with fear, as if the event really were happening.

First, Beck taught his patient to let the image vanish when Beck clapped his hands. Next, he taught the patient to make the image disappear by clapping his own hands.

That accomplished, he taught the patient a technique whereby he could call up the image at will. The patient now felt he had control over the image and was no longer captive to it. When he realized this, the image lost its power and the associated anxiety faded away.

Beck and other therapists have developed another visualization technique which they call "forward time projection." This technique involves visualization of a subject of anxiety, such as a forthcoming medical operation, and the projection of images related to it, into the future. The patient is instructed to see himself or herself six months after the operation, when he or she is well and happy again. This enables him or her to put his fears into perspective and to see that life will go on beyond the crisis of the moment.

Behavioral therapist Joseph Wolpe has invented a technique that works in the opposite way. He has his subjects overcome their fears by visualizing images associated with the cause of their phobias or anxiety.

For example, someone who is afraid of cats is instructed to imagine the least frightening scene he can think of in which cats appear. The resulting image produces a mild level of anxiety which patient and therapist work together to eradicate entirely.

Then they go on to a more anxiety-producing image, until the fear associated with that is similarly eradicated. The process continues, with ever more frightening cat-related images concocted and overcome, until the patient is free of his irrational fears.

CREATING A NEW YOU

The effectiveness of visualization as a method of dealing with psychological problems has long been recognized. Sigmund Freud believed that images were the "language" of the unconscious. "Thinking in pictures ... approximates more closely unconscious processes than does thinking in words," he wrote.

Psychologists and psychiatrists use images in a number of ways. Sometimes they encourage patients to relax, let images arise spontaneously from the unconscious mind, and then interact with these images in some appropriate manner. The great psychologist and philosopher C.G. Jung spent years practicing visualization of his own inner images, describing this period as "the most important in my life."

This sort of unguided free exploration of the unconscious is different from the kind of visualization with which we are concerned. In creative visualization we enter the unconscious in search of a particular something; our quest, in other words, has a specific goal. Most importantly, at all times the conscious mind is in full control, so that we need not worry about being drowned in a flood of unconscious images—a very real danger, since insanity occurs when the unconscious mind overwhelms the conscious.

Creative visualization involves the fashioning of an image in the conscious mind and the charging (and constant recharging) of that image by the enormous psychic energy of the unconscious. We are, in a sense, overwhelmed. But what is really overwhelmed is the resistance our lower selves have to what our higher selves want to be.

Your lower self is that part of your mind which tells you that you are weak, lazy, stupid, unattractive, selfish and generally unworthy. Your lower self seeks instant gratification, living only for the moment and itself. It is amoral and directionless. The more you live inside it and let it determine how you live, the more desperately unhappy you are going to be. The negative images that arise from this will permeate your entire being.

THE HIGHER SELF

The higher self is that part of your psyche which links you with what one writer calls "the supply of

infinite love, wisdom and energy in the universe."
Mystics who have experienced it in its pure form
describe it as a blinding white light. Mystics say the
experience of illumination (also called the "peak
experience" or "cosmic consciousness") causes one
to see the universe and all of humanity as a single
entity bound by limitless love.

This experience has occurred to people in all
places and at all times. One man who experienced
it, Richard Maurice Bucke, described it this way:

> All at once, without warning of any kind, I
> found myself wrapped in a flame-colored
> cloud. For an instant I thought of fire, an
> immense conflagration somewhere close by
> in that great city; the next thing I knew the
> fire was within myself. Directly afterward
> there came upon me a sense of exultation, of
> immense joyousness accompanied or imme-
> diately followed by an intellectual illumina-
> tion impossible to describe. Among other
> things, I did not merely come to believe, but
> I saw that the universe is not composed of
> dead matter, but is, on the contrary, a living
> Presence; I became conscious in myself of
> eternal life. It was not a conviction that I
> would have eternal life, but a consciousness
> that I possessed eternal life then. I saw that
> all men are immortal; that the cosmic order
> is such that without any peradventure all
> things work together for the good of each
> and all; that the foundation principle of the
> world, of all the worlds, is what we call love;
> and that the happiness of each and all is in

the long run absolutely certain. The vision lasted a few seconds and was gone; but the memory of it and the sense of the reality of what it taught has remained during the quarter of a century which has since elapsed.

IN HARMONY WITH THE GREATER REALITY

When we practice visualization, we seek harmony with the world. We see ourselves as benevolent, worthwhile beings who have a place in the universe and whose hopes and dreams can be accomplished there. They can be accomplished because they are right and appropriate, truer than the unhappy distractions and illusions of the moment.

In visualizing, we do not become mystics, of course, but implicitly recognize the truth of the mystical vision. We tap into the same energy mystics experience, but we use it for practical ends. These practical ends are in harmony with the greater reality of love and unity to which our higher self is attuned.

It is hardly coincidental that people who practice visualization regularly find themselves undergoing profound personal transformation. They may have begun their visualization to achieve a rather mundane end—freedom from financial anxiety, for example—but as they continue in the practice of communing with the higher self (which is part of the unconscious), they become better human beings.

They find inner peace and self-understanding, which frees them to love others and to see how their own well-being is tied into the well-being of all. By becoming loving people—and by being seen as loving people—they discover the world opens up to them. When it does, material and spiritual prosperity come together just as the conscious and unconscious minds come together when visualizers envision.

HOW DO YOU DO IT?

Anyone can visualize. The techniques range from the simple to the complex.

But to use them effectively, you have to know how to use them, to be sure you are not wasting your time with wishful thinking and idle fantasizing. Two of the world's leading authorities on visualization have written a fascinating and important book which could change your life.

The Llewellyn Practical Guide to Creative Visualization by Melita Denning and Osborne Phillips tells you how to use your inner resources for "success power." It tells you everything you need to know to turn your life around and to find the success, happiness, health and financial security you seek. It also shows how to draw on psychological, psychic and magical forces for immediate and positive effect.

As Denning and Phillips put it:

> Behind all your visualizing and image-building, giving it validity and meaning, is the reality of Deity; a more real reality than any earthly thing, a Power more powerful and more loving than we can comprehend. If we can only learn to ask aright—and a full trust and a clear perception of our real wants is what is meant here—there is no limit to the abundance, both spiritual and material, with which we shall be blessed.

Happy visualizing!

On the following pages you will find listed, with their current prices, some of the books now available on related subjects. Your book dealer stocks most of these and will stock new titles in the Llewellyn series as they become available. We urge your patronage.

TO GET A FREE CATALOG

To obtain our full catalog, you are invited to write (see address below) for our bi-monthly news magazine/catalog, *Llewellyn's New Worlds of Mind and Spirit*. A sample copy is free, and it will continue coming to you at no cost as long as you are an active mail customer. Or you may subscribe for just $10 in the United States and Canada ($20 overseas, first class mail). Many bookstores also have *New Worlds* available to their customers. Ask for it.

TO ORDER BOOKS AND TAPES

If your book store does not carry the titles described on the following pages, you may order them directly from Llewellyn by sending the full price in U.S. funds, plus postage and handling (see below).

Credit card orders: VISA, MasterCard, American Express are accepted. Call us toll-free within the United States and Canada at 1-800-THE MOON.

Postage and Handling: Include $4 postage and handling for orders $15 and under; $5 for orders *over* $15. There are no postage and handling charges for orders over $100. Postage and handling rates are subject to change. We ship UPS whenever possible within the continental United States; delivery is guaranteed. Please provide your street address as UPS does not deliver to P.O. boxes. Orders shipped to Alaska, Hawaii, Canada, Mexico and Puerto Rico will be sent via first class mail. Allow 4-5 weeks for delivery. International orders: Airmail—add retail price of each book and $5 for each non-book item (audiotapes, etc.); Surface mail - add $1 per item.

Minnesota residents please add 7% sales tax.

Llewellyn Worldwide
P.O. Box 64383-353, St. Paul, MN 55164-0383, U.S.A.

For customer service, call (612) 291-1970

Prices subject to change without notice.

**THE LLEWELLYN PRACTICAL GUIDE
TO CREATIVE VISUALIZATION**
For the Fulfillment of Your Desires
by Denning & Phillips

All things you will ever want must have their start in your mind. The average person uses very little of the full creative power that is his, potentially. It's like the power locked in the atom—it's all there, but you have to learn to release it and apply it constructively.

IF YOU CAN SEE IT … in your Mind's Eye … you will have it! It's true: you can have whatever you want, but there are "laws" to mental creation that must be followed. The power of the mind is not limited to, nor limited by, the material world. *Creative Visualization* enables Man to reach beyond, into the invisible world of Astral and Spiritual Forces.

Some people apply this innate power without actually knowing what they are doing, and achieve great success and happiness; most people, however, use this same power, again unknowingly, incorrectly, and experience bad luck, failure, or at best an unfulfilled life.

This book changes that. Through an easy series of step-by-step, progressive exercises, your mind is applied to bring desire into realization! Wealth, power, success, happiness even psychic powers … even what we call magickal power and spiritual attainment … all can be yours. You can easily develop this completely natural power, and correctly apply it, for your immediate and practical benefit. Illustrated with unique, "puts-you-into-the-picture" visualization aids.

0-87542-183-0, 294 pgs., 5-¼ x 8, illus., softcover $8.95

**THE LLEWELLYN PRACTICAL GUIDE
TO PSYCHIC SELF-DEFENSE AND WELL-BEING
by Denning & Phillips**

Psychic well-being and psychic self-defense are two sides of the same coin, just as are physical health and resistance to disease. Each person (and every living thing) is surrounded by an electromagnetic force field, or Aura, that can provide the means to psychic self-defense and to dynamic well-being. This book explores the world of very real "psychic warfare" of which we are all victims.

Every person in our modern world is subjected to psychic stress and psychological bombardment: advertising promotions that play upon primitive emotions, political and religious appeals that work on feelings of insecurity and guilt, noise, threats of violence and war, news of crime and disaster, etc.

This book shows the nature of genuine psychic attacks—ranging from actual acts of black magic to bitter jealousy and hate—and the reality of psychic stress, the structure of the psyche and its interrelationship with the physical body. It shows how each person must develop his weakened aura into a powerful defense-shield, thereby gaining both physical protection and energetic well-being that can extend to protection from physical violence, accidents and even ill health.

0-87542-190-3, 306 pgs., 5-¼ x 8, illus., softcover $8.95

HOW TO SEE AND READ THE AURA
by Ted Andrews

Everyone has their own aura—the three-dimensional, shapechanging and color changing energy field that surrounds all matter. And anyone can learn to see and experience the aura more effectively. There is nothing magical about the process. It simply involves a little understanding, time, practice and perseverance.

Do some people make you feel drained? Do you find some rooms more comfortable and enjoyable to be in? Have you ever been able to sense the presence of other people before you actually heard or saw them? If so, you have experienced another person's aura. In this practical, easy-to-read manual, you receive a variety of exercises to practice alone and with partners to build your skills in aura reading and interpretation. Also, you will learn to balance your aura each day to keep it vibrant and strong so others cannot drain your vital force.

Learning to see the aura not only breaks down old barriers—it also increases sensitivity. As we develop the ability to see and feel the more subtle aspects of life, our intuition unfolds and increases, and the childlike joy and wonder of life returns.

0-87542-013-3, 160 pgs., mass market, illus. **$3.95**

HOW TO UNCOVER YOUR PAST LIVES
by Ted Andrews

Knowledge of your past lives can be extremely reward-ing. It can assist you in opening to new depths within your own psychological makeup. It can provide greater insight into present circumstances with loved ones, career and health. It is also a lot of fun.

Now Ted Andrews shares with you nine different tech-niques that you can use to access your past lives. Between techniques, Andrews discusses issues such as karma and how it is expressed in your present life; the source of past life information; soul mates and twin souls; proving past lives; the mysteries of birth and death; animals and rein-carnation; abortion and premature death; and the role of reincarnation in Christianity.

To explore your past lives, you need only use one or more of the techniques offered. Complete instructions are provided for a safe and easy regression. Learn to dowse to pinpoint the years and places of your lives with great accuracy, make your own self-hypnosis tape, attune to the incoming child during pregnancy, use the tarot and the cabala in past life meditations, keep a past life journal and more.

0-87542-022-2, 240 pgs., mass market, illus. **$3.95**

THE SECRET OF LETTING GO
by Guy Finley

Whether you need to let go of a painful heartache, a destructive habit, a frightening worry or a nagging discontent, *The Secret of Letting Go* shows you how to call upon your own hidden powers and how they can take you through and beyond any challenge or problem. This book reveals the secret source of a brand-new kind of inner strength.

In the light of your new and higher self-understanding, emotional difficulties such as loneliness, fear, anxiety and frustration fade into nothingness as you happily discover they never really existed in the first place.

With a foreword by Desi Arnaz Jr., and introduction by Dr. Jesse Freeland, *The Secret of Letting Go* is a pleasing balance of questions and answers, illustrative examples, truth tales, and stimulating dialogues that allow the reader to share in the exciting discoveries that lead up to lasting self-liberation.

This is a book for the discriminating, intelligent, and sensitive reader who is looking for *real* answers.

0-87542-223-3, 240 pgs., 5-¼ x 8, softcover $9.95

FREEDOM FROM THE TIES THAT BIND
The Secret of Self Liberation
by Guy Finley

Imagine how your life would flow *without* the weight of those weary inner voices constantly convincing you that "you can't," or complaining that someone else should be blamed for the way *you* feel. The weight of the world on your shoulders would be replaced by a bright, new sense of freedom. Fresh, new energies would flow. *You could choose to live the way* YOU *want.* In *Freedom from the Ties that Bind*, Guy Finley reveals hundreds of Celestial, but down-to-earth, secrets of Self-Liberation that show you exactly how to be fully independent, and *free of any condition not to your liking.* Even the most difficult people won't be able to turn your head or test your temper. Enjoy solid, meaningful relationships founded *in conscious choice*—not *through self-defeating compromise.* Learn the secrets of unlocking the door to your own Free Mind. Be empowered to break free of any self-punishing pattern, and make the discovery that who you really are is already everything you've ever wanted to be.

0-87542-217-9, 240 pgs., 6 x 9, softbound $10.00

THE LLEWELLYN DEEP MIND TAPE
FOR ASTRAL PROJECTION
by Denning & Phillips

The authors of *The Llewellyn Practical Guide to Astral Projection* are adepts fully experienced in all levels of psychic development and training. They have designed this ninety-minute cassette tape to guide you through full relaxation and all the preparations for projection.

With the added dimension of the author's personally produced electronic synthesizer patterns of sound and music, they program the Deep Mind through the stages of awakening, and projection of the astral Body of Light. And then the programming guides your safe return to normal consciousness with memory—enabling you to bridge the worlds of Body, Mind and Spirit.

The Deep Mind Tape is a powerful new technique combining guided Mind Programming with specially created sound and music to evoke deep level response in the psyche and its psychic centers for controlled development, and induction of the Out-of-Body Experience.

0-87542-168-7, 90 minute cassette tape $9.95

HOW TO HEAL WITH COLOR
by Ted Andrews

Now, for perhaps the first time, color therapy is placed within the grasp of the average individual. Anyone can learn to facilitate and accelerate the healing process on all levels with the simple color therapies discussed in *How to Heal with Color.*

Color serves as a vibrational remedy that interacts with the human energy system to stabilize physical, emotional, mental and spiritual conditions. When there is balance, we can more effectively rid ourselves of toxins, negativities and patterns that hinder our life processes.

This book provides color application guidelines that are beneficial for over 50 physical conditions and a wide variety of emotional and mental conditions. Receive simple and tangible instructions for performing "muscle testing" on yourself and others to find the most beneficial colors. Learn how to apply color therapy through touch, projection, breathing, cloth, water and candles. Learn how to use the little known but powerful color-healing system of the mystical Qabala to balance and open the psychic centers. Plus, discover simple techniques for performing long distance healings on others.

0-87542-005-2, 240 pgs., mass market, illus. $4.99